CURIOUS PET PALS

MY FRIEND THE POTBELLIED PIG

JOANNE RANDOLPH

WINDMILL BOOKS
New York

Published in 2011 by Windmill Books, LLC
303 Park Avenue South, Suite # 1280, New York, NY 10010-3657

First Edition

Editor: Jennifer Way
Book Design: Erica Clendening
Layout Design: Julio Gil
Photo Researcher: Greg Tucker

Photo Credits: Cover, p. 12–13 Karl Schatz/Getty Images; pp. 4, 6, 7 (top), 8, 9,14, 15, 19, 21 Shutterstock.com; p. 5 © www.iStockphoto.com/Nancy Nehring; p. 7 (bottom) WILDLIFE/Peter Arnold Inc.; pp. 10, 18 Stan Honda/AFP/Getty Images; pp. 11 (top), 20 Frank Brandel/AFP/Getty Images; p. 11 (bottom) David Hecker/AFP/Getty Images; p. 16 Westend61/Getty Images; p. 17 © www.iStockphoto.com/Olaf Bender.

Library of Congress Cataloging-in-Publication Data

Randolph, Joanne.
  My friend the potbellied pig / by Joanne Randolph.
     p. cm. — (Curious pet pals)
  Includes index.
  ISBN 978-1-60754-975-8 (library binding) — ISBN 978-1-60754-982-6 (pbk.) — ISBN 978-1-60754-983-3 (6-pack)
  1. Potbellied pigs as pets—Juvenile literature. I. Title.
  SF393.P47R36 2011
  636.4'85—dc22
                                        2010004694

Manufactured in the United States of America

For more great fiction and nonfiction, go to www.windmillbooks.com.

CPSIA Compliance Information: Batch #BW2011WM: For Further Information contact Rosen Publishing, New York, New York at 1-800-237-9932

CONTENTS

When you think of pigs, you may think of huge animals that live on farms. These animals are not

FARM PIG

house pets. A farm pig can weigh more than 1,000 pounds (454 kg). You may not want that much pig in your living room!

Potbellied pig babies, or piglets, are very cute. However, it is important to find out what potbellied pigs are like before you take one into your family.

Potbellied pigs can make great pets, though. Potbellied pigs are also called Vietnamese potbellied pigs. They became a popular pet in the United States around 1985.

5

Pigs are smart, clean, and loving animals. These sound like the characteristics of a great pet. Potbellied pigs are not the ideal pet for every family, however.

This potbellied pig has been trained to walk on a leash.

Raising and caring for a potbellied pig takes work, patience, and training. It can be a big job to care for a potbellied pig,

These pigs are grazing, or eating grass.

just like it is for any pet. If you put the time in, these pets can make great friends!

Pigs can be loving members of a family. It is important to train your pig and get it used to children and other pets, though.

Potbellied pigs get their name because they have a round belly. The first potbellied pigs that were

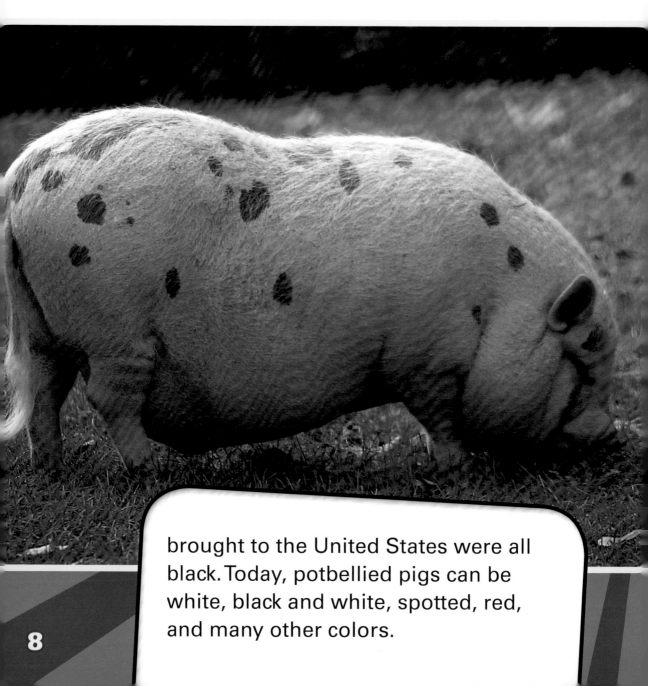

brought to the United States were all black. Today, potbellied pigs can be white, black and white, spotted, red, and many other colors.

This round belly does not mean the pig is overweight. This is just how potbellied pigs look!

Although they are smaller than farm pigs, potbellied pigs are not small. A potbellied pig can weigh up to 175 pounds (79 kg)! Most potbellied pigs grow up to be about as heavy as a medium-sized dog.

IN OR OUT?

Potbellied pigs can make good indoor pets. However, you will want to pig-**proof** your home first.

These potbellied pigs are happily spending time outside.

How do you pig-proof your home? You need to move your belongings, such as papers, bags, and shoes, out of the potbellied pig's reach.

This pig likely enjoys its life inside with its owners. Even indoor potbellied pigs need time outside, though.

Pigs like to explore and eat, and your pig may try to munch on your things! Give your pig its own toys and chews. This will help **encourage** it to leave your things alone.

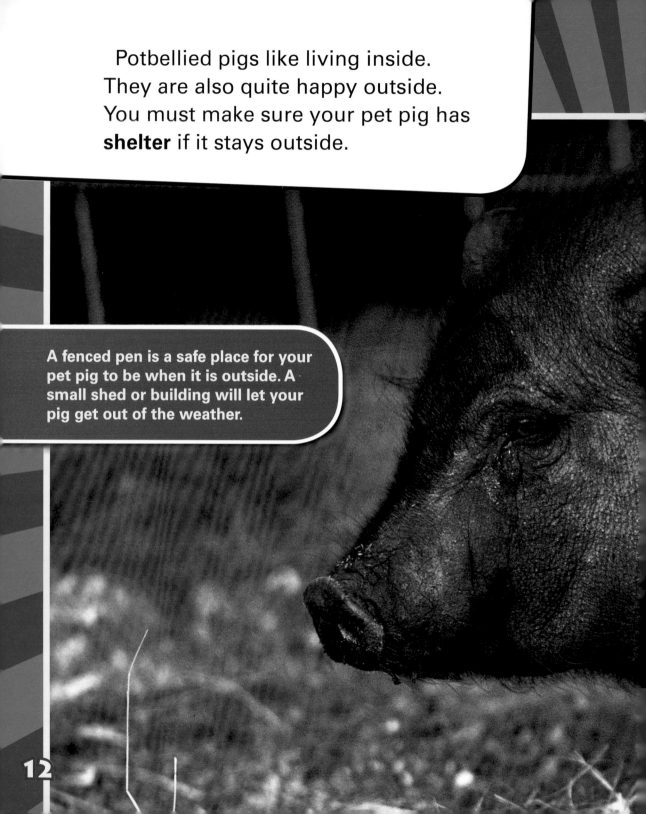

Potbellied pigs like living inside. They are also quite happy outside. You must make sure your pet pig has **shelter** if it stays outside.

A fenced pen is a safe place for your pet pig to be when it is outside. A small shed or building will let your pig get out of the weather.

A small shed or other place will keep your pig safe from wind and weather. Its pen should also be safe from **predators**, such as dogs and wild animals.

No matter where your pig lives, it may be happiest with other pig friends. This way your pig can spend time **socializing** with other pigs.

Pigs are very clean animals. This means they do not need to be bathed often. They will sometimes

Pigs like to roll around in the mud in hot weather. This keeps bugs away and keeps their skin safe from the sun.

need a bath, though. You can use a small child's swimming pool or the tub for baths.

TUSK

Potbellied pigs also need to have their **hooves** clipped, or cut, each year. Male pigs grow **tusks**. After the pig is about 2 years old, your vet may need to cut the tusks back.

Pigs can be bossy. Potbellied pigs are no different. They are used to living in groups where

Rewarding good behavior is the best way to end up with a well-trained, trusting pig. Rewards can be food treats, toys, or extra love.

one pig is the leader. Sometimes the pigs push each other around or fight to decide who is the lead pig.

Pigs that live in barns like to sleep on straw or wood shavings.

You need to let your pig know you are the leader in your family. This does not mean you should be mean to your pig. Instead, you need to train your pig to give you the **behavior** you want.

You are probably not surprised to learn that pigs like to eat! Potbellied pigs like lots of different foods.

This potbellied pig is munching on lettuce.

You should feed them food that is made for potbellied pigs. You can get this special food at a pet store.

Carrots are healthy food for potbellied pigs.

You can also give potbellied pigs vegetables as treats. Some favorite vegetables are celery, cucumbers, carrots, and greens. Offer healthy food choices to your pet. If you do, you will have a healthy pig!

Potbellied pigs are not the easiest pet to have. No pet is truly easy. Caring for any animal is a big job.

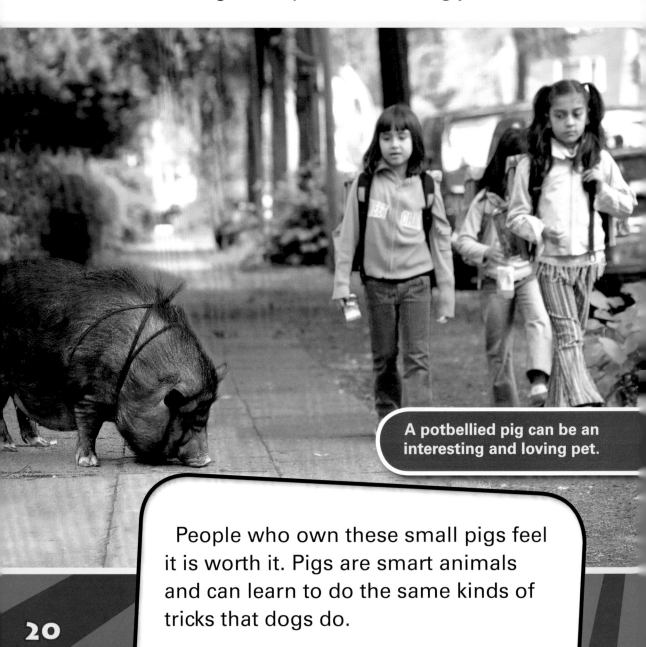

A potbellied pig can be an interesting and loving pet.

People who own these small pigs feel it is worth it. Pigs are smart animals and can learn to do the same kinds of tricks that dogs do.

If your pig uses a litter box, fill it with wood shavings and not cat litter.

With a little time and patience, they end up with a loving, smart, playful friend! Are you ready to bring a potbellied pig home?

GUESS WHAT?

Pigs cannot see very well, but they have great senses of smell and hearing. Pigs smell so well that they are used to find a special kind of mushroom, called a truffle.

Police officers sometimes use potbellied pigs to smell for drugs or bombs.

Foods that are good for training pet pigs are raisins, apples, and grapes. These foods should only be fed to pigs in small amounts.

Female potbellied pigs are called sows. Males are called boars. Babies are called piglets.

Potbellied pigs can live for anywhere from 12 to 20 years.

Potbellied pigs keep growing until they are about 4 years old.

GLOSSARY

BEHAVIOR (bee-HAY-vyur) Ways to act.

ENCOURAGE (in-KUR-ij) To give someone reason to do something.

HOOVES (HOOVZ) The hard coverings on the feet of certain animals.

PREDATORS (PREH-duh-terz) Animals that kill other animals for food.

PROOF (PROOF) Able to withstand or be kept safe against.

SHELTER (SHEL-ter) A place that guards someone or something from weather or danger.

SOCIALIZING (SOH-shuh-lyz-ing) Seeking out the company of fellow animal and learning to be friendly with them.

TUSKS (TUSKS) Long, large pointed teeth that come out of the mouths of some animals.

READ MORE

Orr, Tamra. *How to Convince Your Parents You Can Care For a Potbellied Pig.* Hockessin, DE: Mitchell Lane Publishers, 2008.

Tait, Leia. *Potbellied Pig.* New York: Weigl Publishing, 2006.

Lunis, Natalie. *Potbellied Pigs.* New York: Bearport Publishing, 2009.

INDEX

WEB SITES

For Web resources related to the subject of this book, go to: www.windmillbooks.com/weblinks and select this book's title.